Neglected Aspects of Sufi Study

Books by Idries Shah

Sufi Studies and Middle Eastern Literature
The Sufis
Caravan of Dreams
The Way of the Sufi
Tales of the Dervishes: *Teaching-stories Over a Thousand Years*
Sufi Thought and Action

**Traditional Psychology,
Teaching Encounters and Narratives**
Thinkers of the East: *Studies in Experientialism*
Wisdom of the Idiots
The Dermis Probe
Learning How to Learn: *Psychology and Spirituality in the Sufi Way*
Knowing How to Know
The Magic Monastery: *Analogical and Action Philosophy*
Seeker After Truth
Observations
Evenings with Idries Shah
The Commanding Self

University Lectures
A Perfumed Scorpion (Institute for the Study of Human Knowledge and California University)
Special Problems in the Study of Sufi Ideas (Sussex University)
The Elephant in the Dark: *Christianity, Islam and the Sufis* (Geneva University)
Neglected Aspects of Sufi Study: *Beginning to Begin* (The New School for Social Research)
Letters and Lectures of Idries Shah

Current and Traditional Ideas
Reflections
The Book of the Book
A Veiled Gazelle: *Seeing How to See*
Special Illumination: *The Sufi Use of Humor*

The Mulla Nasrudin Corpus
The Pleasantries of the Incredible Mulla Nasrudin
The Subtleties of the Inimitable Mulla Nasrudin
The Exploits of the Incomparable Mulla Nasrudin
The World of Nasrudin

Travel and Exploration
Destination Mecca

Studies in Minority Beliefs
The Secret Lore of Magic
Oriental Magic

Selected Folktales and Their Background
World Tales

A Novel
Kara Kush

Sociological Works
Darkest England
The Natives Are Restless
The Englishman's Handbook

Translated by Idries Shah
The Hundred Tales of Wisdom (Aflaki's *Munaqib*)

Neglected Aspects of Sufi Study

"Beginning to Begin"

Idries Shah

ISF PUBLISHING

Copyright © The Estate of Idries Shah

The right of the Estate of Idries Shah to be identified
as the owner of this work has been asserted by them in accordance
with the Copyright, Designs and Patents Act 1988.

All rights reserved
Copyright throughout the world

ISBN 978-1-78479-286-2

First published 1977
Published in this edition 2017

No part of this publication may be reproduced or transmitted in
any form or by any means, electronic, mechanical or photographic,
by recording or any information storage or retrieval system or
method now known or to be invented or adapted, without prior
permission obtained in writing from the publisher, ISF Publishing,
except by a reviewer quoting brief passages in a review written for
inclusion in a journal, magazine, newspaper, blog or broadcast.

Requests for permission to reprint, reproduce etc., to:
The Permissions Department
ISF Publishing
The Idries Shah Foundation
P. O. Box 71911
London NW2 9QA
United Kingdom
permissions@isf-publishing.org

In association with The Idries Shah Foundation

The Idries Shah Foundation is a registered charity in the
United Kingdom
Charity No. 1150876

IDRIES SHAH

NEGLECTED ASPECTS OF SUFI STUDY*

On the Nature of Sufi Knowledge

* Based on lectures at the New School for Social Research, New York, and the University of California, San Francisco, in association with the Institute for the Study of Human Knowledge, Stanford, California, May 1976.

NEGLECTED ASPECTS OF SUFI STUDY

On the Nature of Sufi Knowledge

The Role of Systematization – Interpretation of Poetry – Scholarship as distinct from Knowledge – Disturbance caused by Outwardness – "Polishing the Mirror" – The Apparent as the Bridge to the Real – The Consistency of Inconsistency – Cults as barriers to Wisdom – Disabling effects of Emotion – Testing the Tested – What kind of Experience? – Using Current methods of Research – The role of Assumptions – Historical instance of scholars arraigning a Sufi "heresy" – The difference between studying ABOUT Sufism and IN Sufism – How Sufis can be understood in the West – The Immature Self – Three Methods of Study – Teaching-Stories – Why does a joke wear out? – A Reality without a Name, or a Name without a Reality? – Eastern ideas in Western settings – Fragmentation of Teachings – Experience, Qualities and Capacity – Extra-Normal Experiences – Dilution of Method – The Primary Tasks – The use of exercises, music, dance, song, costume, names – Mutual recognition of Sufis – Ritualistic practice – Extradimensional Cognition – A Framework for New Knowledge – The Completed Human Being – Reason for so many Sufi schools – "The Secret Preserves Itself" – Seeing and Knowing – Conditioning, Anxiety, Impatience – What the Teacher should make clear – Pitfalls in Study – The Emergence of the Learning Function – How everything fits into its Place.

You may have forgotten the Way:
But those who came before
Did not forget you.
> *Saying of Master Bahaudin
> Naqshband of Bokhara*

On the Nature of Sufi Knowledge

IN A COLLECTION of the Quatrains of Omar ibn Ibrahim al-Khayyam we find this poem:

> Chun hasil i adami dar in shuristan
> Juz khurdan i ghussa nist, ya kandan i jan
> Khurram dil i anki z'in jahan zud biraft
> Asuda kasi ki khud niyamad bajahan

> Since the lot of humankind in this bitter land
> Is nothing but suffering and sadness
> Happy the heart of whoever quickly leaves the world –
> Tranquil the person who did not come at all

But, since we are all here, and haven't now the option of not coming at all, we deal with it as it is....

I cannot, and I am sure that you would not want me to, use what is usually termed a systematic approach at this juncture. This is, of course, because Sufism is always systematized only for limited or transitory periods: because Sufism is primarily instrumental, not for enjoyment or display. But its study, especially in poetry, can be hard. In Khayyam's quatrain, the first line refers to the problems of study (hard if we take it on that level); annoyance and disappointment come during the studies, as in the second line. The third line refers to the happiness of rapid or temporary "leaving the world," sometimes found in ecstatic experiences, but it is not permanent. The last line speaks of "whoever did not come at all" as the state of whoever is not burdened by the considerations which prevent his perception of objectivity: of the untrammeled knowledge of the "original," or, in another formulation, of the "realized" or "returned" man or woman – returned to the essential state of knowledge or objective Truth.

So, if you have been through certain stages of learning, you can discern, underlying the poetry, the humor and the emotional aspects, the pattern of the stages through which people pass in their Sufi journey or process. Approaching the materials analytically requires the right kind of analysis.

Were it otherwise than that Sufi development is experience, you would be able to get all your knowledge from books, as with other subjects of human study where exemplars, demonstrators, practitioners and living teachers are not needed. There would be very little need for "live" lectures, and people could read papers or hear talks through recordings or the printed word alone.

This is not to say that Sufi knowledge does not take advantage of books, though on a lower level. Since we live in a highly literate and literary culture, books and even transmissions of knowledge *can* be useful, providing only that one knows how to use them. Because, I suppose, of a yearning for personal contact, people have often leapt upon my saying that knowledge comes from a person and not from a book, demanding "teachings" and refusing books. This has been reinforced, through the well-known habit of selective reading, by quotations from Rumi, such as, in the *Diwani Shams i Tabriz*, when he says, of the Man of God:

Mard i Khuda nist faqih az kitab

The Man of God is not a scholar from
a book

The would-be students wish to transcend books.

But, ask yourselves: if someone says that books do not contain wisdom, and yet he writes books; books do not contain Sufism, and yet he continues to publish books on Sufism, what is really happening? It really is your duty, and not mine, to ask and to find the answer to that question, if you are interested enough. But, since we are here and it has come up, let us answer it to illustrate the way of thinking which is so important to us.

First of all, hear Sheikh Saadi, where he writes, in the second chapter of the *Gulistan*, the "Rose Garden":

> Batil ast an ki mudda'ai guyad
> "Khufta ra khufta kai kunad bedar?"
> Mard bayad ki girad andar gush
> War nawisht pand bar diwar.

Eastwick translates this as:

> Futile is the objector's scorning
> "Sleepers ope not slumber's eye."
> Heed then well the words of warning
> Though on a wall thou them descry.

This may sound like poetry, but if we translate it for *content*, more literally and less rhythmically, we get in English:

> It is vain, what the accuser may say:
> "When can the sleeper awaken the sleeper?"
> Humanity must get it into the ear, even if it is written wisdom on a wall.

NEGLECTED ASPECTS OF SUFI STUDY

The two conceptions do not conflict. They do, if we are dealing with literal thinkers who imagine that they are studying a form of, say, physics where everything must always be the same. What they forget constitutes two of the most significant items in Sufi study:

1. Circumstances alter cases. Advice given at one time may not apply at another, or for another person.
2. The poem tells us that certain things must be heard, even if they are written down. The poet does not say – and do you not imagine that he was capable of saying it? – what Eastwick imagines. He does not say: "Tell people things even if they are not listening." Neither does he say: "Wherever you get this information, it is important." It actually says that whatever form it appears in, it must get into another form when being absorbed. It does not say, for instance, "Even if you are asleep, you must hear it"; or "Even if it is on a wall you must see it." The first two lines are not necessarily intended to explain the second two – unless you are working on the low level which was the height of Eastwick's capacity, or perhaps the height of what he thought his readers could

take. The unlocking of the meaning of a poem comes through contemplation, not enjoyment, in this kind of instance. And this is not a criticism of enjoyment, merely of incomplete working with the material. So, with written materials, things written down can provoke thought, can increase focus in directions where perceptions can operate on a higher level. It may be written on the wall. It must get into the ear. These are analogies which mean: "They come in through one perception, they are assimilated by another. They may be presented in more than one way or locution." Much Sufi literature is analogical or provocative. It is intended to cause you to do or feel something. That something is not confined to like or dislike, to hope or fear, to cudgeling your brains, to discussing with your friends. These customary ways of dealing with almost anything merely mask the developmental, the educational, content. And, before one gets to that point, things which have been read leave a trace. This trace, not necessarily consciously registered by the "sleeper," will be digested into another area when adequate experiences are operating.

NEGLECTED ASPECTS OF SUFI STUDY

At this point, people very often say: "This is terribly difficult," or "This is not what I came for." The answer, of course, is that this is the difficulty characteristic of Sufi study: just as the difficulty characteristic of Zen study might be to imagine a clap with one hand, or, with certain forms of monastic discipline, to flagellate oneself. Before you think that something is too difficult, ask yourself whether other things are any easier.

The nature of Sufi knowledge is that it has an outward shape, constantly reformulated to make it more accessible and to maintain contact with the culture in which it operates, and it has an inward meaning, which it is the task of the school and the teacher to bring to the student, with both parties exercising maximum effort – maximum relevant effort. Remember: one man's relevance is another man's nonsense. Most people work only on the outside. It is neater, but does it help?

In the London *Times* the other day, it was recorded that a semi-official British organization – the British Council, a cultural body – has been baffling its pensionaries with instructions printed on their sealed payment envelopes. The notice reads:

> IMPORTANT – if the envelope contains money, check the amount *before*

opening. Claims for shortage will not be considered if the staple or flap have been disturbed.

I am all for flaps not being disturbed: but what about *people* being disturbed by externalist thinking like this? Those of us who are engaged in the matter of Sufism often feel that people trying to approach the subject want, however unwittingly, to divine the contents from the outside, what some call the lowest level. They want the contents without opening the container; want, that is, to understand the subject without entering enough into it. So I must reaffirm, following with apologies for any unfashionability but without any personal reluctance, the admonition of the Sufis for centuries that Sufism is studied by Sufis and by Sufi methods. Anything short of this is sure to provide a more or less simplified picture, subject to limitations of understanding, unless at the same time the door is kept open for a further range of understanding.

The removal, transformation or outmaneuvering of those misunderstandings about Sufism, which are so prevalent today among cultists and even some of the conventionally learned – as they have always been prevalent – this dealing with the underbrush, remains one of the most important tasks of the Sufi. You will realize how important when I say that Sufis such as Ibn Arabi (The Greatest Sheikh) insisted that Sufi knowledge was adequately represented as enabling people to understand the knowledge which they already had, by "polishing the mirror" of their minds. This means that it is as adequately represented in this manner as in the other way of referring to it as the developing faculties. Sufism is experiential. Capacities, even those for learning beyond a certain point, are provoked by Sufis, by one's own efforts and what results from them, and by an element of what is referred to by Sufis as the Divine.

Sufism is experience, and hence not to be defined – imprisoned – in perennial, static categories. Sufis never tire of saying this. Because most ordinary thinkers, those accustomed to conventionalized thought, do not study Sufism and *also* take this contention into account, they generally ignore it. In so doing, of course, they provide the hilarious sight of people who purport to explain Sufism, often to intermesh it with various religious, mystical, or occult systems (sometimes all three) in books, articles, lectures, but do it violence by including in their rendition of Sufism only such arguments and other materials as enable them to work in this way. What has happened here is rather as if a knitter of string shopping bags has unpicked a carpet and taken the hessian, sackcloth, warp or woof and made a bag out of it. It may be useful in this form for the transportation of groceries and other things, but it should not now be called "a carpet," or "what a carpet should really look like." You can buy books by such people at almost any bookstore in the Western world these days. Some writers in the East also produce them, and certain publishers in the East publish some of them. All of this leads to much confusion.

But there are other people than these. First, there are those, not so few in numbers as some observers imagine, who can and do follow the Sufi thread through materials issuing from authentic Sufi origins and activities. Since such people are not in need of lectures on what Sufism is and is not, we are not talking about them just now. There are others, too, who may or may not have a potentiality to understand things beyond the relatively narrow range now occupied by civilized and cultured man. They often ask: "If virtually all Sufism is experience, and if all Sufi experience is in some way at least unique, how can we study, much less understand, such a phenomenon?"

We do so in exactly the same way as we do other subjects, when we have to introduce a relatively false concept, an approximation, to lead to a truer one; following the maxim *Al-Majazu qantarat al-Haqiqa* – "The Apparent is the Bridge to the Real."

As a rough approximation, we can compare the invariable approach to Sufic study with how we start from the known to the unknown, in conveying, say, "roundness." We say, "the full moon is round, so is a penny, so too is a saucer or plate." All these statements are relatively true, though they may all be said to be relatively false. But perhaps "roundness" is ultimately conveyed, either by this method or by including this method in our attempts to establish it in the mind of the learner. Naturally, according to the experience and other characteristics of the learner, we use different analogies (cake, sun, circle), not forgetting that we must maintain the knowledge of the fact expressed by the proverb:

Every round thing is not a cake.

The barriers to Sufi knowledge, at least initially, are mainly mistaken postures on the part of the student.

The very human desire for consistency, reassurance, certainty, whether these things are useful at any given time, or even if they are positively contra indicated factors at various junctures, causes people – whether approaching Sufism or many other things – to seek, almost to crave, single, definite, very often oversimplified formulae, not as instruments or vehicles of learning, but as "truths." This is the sole reason why temporary teaching formulations (equivalent to "cakes are round") are adopted as "holy writ" or "infallible truths." What has happened is that the individual, whose need for mental stabilization may be stronger than his desire for truth, attaches himself to so-called principles not originally intended to be such. Everyone is familiar with examples of this, even if he or she has not yet identified it in operation within our own Sufi interest.

In many cases this tendency leads to a cult, sometimes literally so, sometimes in a concealed way. As soon as we see the operation of this factor, we have to realize that the individual or group manifesting it is blocked; not seeking Sufi knowledge but equilibrated on a perhaps useful, but effectively different, activity. An example of this behavior is the worship of the "fact." "Such and such a thing is true [under these circumstances] therefore it must always be true; truth is truth and indivisible." With modern science, including physics, discovering rather unequivocally the relative nature of even the most enduring-seeming facts, Sufi thought has a great attraction nowadays and a chance to explain itself a little better. Nowadays it appears to many people far less improbable or magical. A quantity and variety of people can now approach it who, in earlier years, would not have been able to do so "because of its inconsistencies."

In the more specific sense of a cult, of course, Sufi studies have often deteriorated into the automatic and mimetic use of robes, beards, formulae and appurtenances. These exterior objects and concepts have a powerful appeal for those who need reassurance or who desire something strange. But their use without an understanding of any function which they might have or might have had, and the transitory nature of formulation designed to protect and conduct from one stage to another, leads to "idolatry": the grasping and holding onto things which hamper progress because they are static. This is not a Sufi "Way" at all, but a social phenomenon. At best we have a new tribe, at worst a coercive (either/or) instrument.

Saadi refers to this when he says, in Persian:

Ba-Tasbih o sajjah o dalq nist

(The Path) is not in observance
The rosary, the prayer-rug and the robe
(Bostan I)

This is of course what Shabistari (AD 1317) means when he says in *The Secret Garden*, which is much quoted in Sufi circles:

> If the Muslim knew what the idol was / He would know that there is religion in idol-worship / If the polytheist were informed on religion / How could he stray in his faith? / He sees in the idol only the outward and created / For that he is legally a heathen.*

The above passages, inevitably, have been taken by the various self-styled "experts" on Sufism to prove that the Sufis are against religion, or that they are soft on idolaters, and so on, and that "Sufi knowledge" is therefore sophistry. I hope that I do not have to take it that my present audience needs any further interpretation of what these lines mean, viewed from the real Sufi standpoint.

People tend to assume, I am sure you will agree, that because they are emotionally stirred by something, this thing must be of great importance; and also not infrequently that all kinds of prior

---

* Persian text in my *Special Problems in the Study of Sufi Ideas* (Sussex University Seminar 1966), 1974 edition, p. 32, note 93, London.

assumptions about that thing must be correct. They are also often likely to think that because they have external evidence of a thing (including Sufi literature, history and procedures, sometimes for example those called ritual) they can form an accurate picture of what the internal dimensions and origins are. But, if you see people enjoying, say, classical Chinese music, you can perhaps confirm from observing them that this is happening: but without participation and experience of it you cannot feel the same way about it. And this is true on the lower level of an acquired taste.

The emotionally stirred people, of course, include the sincere – confused – as well as the hypocritical imitators of Sufism. The intellectually active include many self-appointed experts on Sufism whose addiction to academic and literary forms, and often to local areas of the world, gives them no real help in their studies, whether they know it or not. The person who really wants to know about Sufism will follow them at his peril. Admittedly the peril is not great; one only risks ending up like them, not knowing very much. But from the point of view of someone who believes that he might understand Sufism, this consolation prize can surely not be worthwhile. Anyway, both the emotionally stirred and the intellectually active, apart from special cases such as phlegmatic people who may have to be stirred (which is why

Rumi instituted Dervish whirling and music, as he informs us, for the local people of a part of Asiatic Turkey), tend to arrive at and to reproduce distortions. Both are (and perhaps always have been) the major public sources of general and even what often passes for specialized information on Sufis and Sufism. Each lacks the essential element, the real Sufi experience. Since I first started to say this, by the way, some of these people, unable to answer the contention otherwise, have started to claim that they have indeed had this experience. It is interesting that they have adapted in this way, because before anyone challenged them publicly they were happy enough to claim that they did not need it.

Sufism as such does not purport to explain human life or to provide a system in which everyone can live in order to become reconciled with their problems. It does, on the other hand, claim that there is a far more objective knowledge and reality than usually imagined, and that Sufi activity can lead to this knowledge, other things being equal. It is when the knowledge has been gained that the problems and the purport of human life are understood. This involves our asking which of us is really putting the cart before the horse.

The situation has not changed since Jalaluddin Rumi seven hundred years ago presented the tale of the travelers who were quarrelling. The Turkish traveler wanted Üzüm, the Greek Staphyl, the Arab 'Ināb. An interpreter stopped the fight by taking their one piece of silver and satisfying them all, since each in his own language sought the same thing – grapes. But that objective knowledge must be there, say the Sufis. If the travelers are not even arguing, and they think that they can work out the problem for themselves... well, it has not been done yet, and I can quote you Saadi on the question:

Ta tiriyaq az Iraq awarda shavad, mar-gazida murda shavad.

"Before the snake serum is brought from Iraq, the snake-bitten one will be dead." And, as the Persian proverb pithily has it:

Āzmuda-ra āzmudan jahl ast.

To test the tested is ignorance.

People who object that they know their own problems and seek only answers to them in the terms in which they present them may very well not be candidates for Sufi study. Paradoxically, it is the very habit of worrying that sometimes brings people to the door of the Sufi, seeking resolution of problems; and yet this worrying tendency may be the first thing which this man or woman has to overcome, or shed, before he or she can benefit from Sufi activity. It is a matter of almost everyday experience for many Sufis that they have to repeat: "The donkey which brought you to this door must be dismissed if you want to get through it."

There is no shortage of encounters on record where people have sought Sufis to resolve their problems and have eventually found that they cannot benefit from Sufi teaching, or perhaps even the "problem-solving service," until they have overcome or resolved certain basic agitations. It is also interesting to observe, on the ground as it were, how people fall into two categories in this respect. Many people seek Sufism mainly because they hope that it will benefit them in the sense of reducing their worries. If the Sufi (or some extraneous cause) helps to remove the problem, many of them discover that they do not "need" Sufism at all! Nobody can spend much time among Sufis with applicants coming in all the time, without noting this striking fact. The Sufi, be it noted, is not just an archaic kind of psychotherapist, as some people – trying desperately to fit traditional thought into present-day categories – would have us believe. The Sufi often enough knows a psychiatric case when he sees one, certainly as well as the next person: and he knows what he himself is supposed to be doing in such a regard.

So Sufism is not based on such things as accepting other people's beliefs about the importance of their feeling of this and that kind. It is not a matter of psychotherapy as presently understood. It is not arbitrary theory – speculation – nor idealism, nor hopefulness that if we think and do certain things, all will be well (what I call magical thinking). How does it work?

First of all, since we are talking about the nature of Sufi knowledge: to be a Sufi is to have experience. A Sufi teacher (not all Sufis are teachers) is one who has "gone beyond" ordinary limits and has become aware of a reality which enables him to see humanity's general and specific condition and other matters in relation to this greater dimension. This we may roughly render as being equivalent to looking at something from the ground and being able to fly or hover over it. This reperception of the world may enable the teacher to guide others to where he "is." That is why it is said that he not only knows the answers to questions but also knows what the real questions are. Because he is also human ("In the world but not OF it"), he can understand the barriers to perception which exist from time to time, and in a certain flow, in the minds of others. Hence the words: "The Guide to the Way who, having been there before, can conduct his student to the destination."

It is perhaps characteristic of the hyperliterary culture in which we live that so many researchers should attempt to discover the Way by an intensive examination of Sufi writings. Today, as never before, books, articles, monographs, based on Sufi texts are everywhere. But, as one Sufi said to me recently, "Egyptologists, however erudite, cannot become Pharaohs. Their students cannot even become pyramid-building slaves – which is just as well!" But every action has, on this planet, a reaction. Perhaps as many people as have ransacked the classics have reacted against this kind of thing and instead tried to become Sufis by mimesis. They will collect a number of practices and formulae and, like sorcerers' apprentices, try to make something work by what in effect, if not in intention, amounts to trying conjurations.

Not long ago I met a scholar who pumped my hand and enthused: "I am delighted to meet you, because I wrote my doctoral thesis on Sufism and you are the first Sufi I have met." I sent him along to a miscellaneous crew of emotionalists who caper around doing "Dervish exercises," and he is now very happy. He was not too sure that his researches had been complete (being on the literary level) and now he is sure that he is "fulfilled." So fulfilled, in fact, that he has to pour some of it out to me in incoherent letters of up to 24 pages, and this has come about in only a few months.

The Sufi saying is that everything which enters the environment of our physics, "that which comes into the world," partakes of its disabilities, loses something, may become distorted. Thus if any idea is given out, some will seize it for profit, others to make a social form out of it, some will deify it and others will fight or amend it, and so on. The materials employed in the pursuit of Sufi experience are no exception.

The culture prevailing at the moment, enriched by the insights of psychology, anthropology and sociology, is far better able than many others to observe these abuses and warping tendencies at work. The only regret is that so many people, at the same time, are so conditioned by the commercial society that a somewhat automatistic mentality prevails. It is very common to receive letters or visits from people who only want "the name and address of my neighborhood enfranchised Sufi teacher." This conjures up in my mind's eye, also obeying the association of ideas tendency, of course, a picture of a sort of Santa Claus in every town.... Unhappily, further correspondence or conversation with such people only too often shows that they are thinking like that, too.

The Sufi path to Truth, then, has certain requirements. It needs the presence of someone who has gone that path before. It requires the existence of people who really want to tread that path. It cannot be followed unless certain environmental factors are included and – just as important – certain others excluded.

It is worth considering exactly what the present interest in Sufism would like to find out, and what methods it is proposed to adopt, and what materials and individuals it is intended should be examined by the people currently engaged in approaching Sufism. First we have the traditional scholars. Somewhat overtaken by events, since a larger amount of Sufi materials and interpretations has been circulating recently, they often tend to continue to work with superseded materials and to vie with one another in the usual scholarly manner. Their historical and textual compilations and criticisms, while sometimes impeccable in their own way, still labor under the difficulty that they cannot afford to throw out anything imagined to be useful in determining, say, chronology; or which they feel represents the working of a given Sufi's mind. And yet they do not mind cutting out materials which are to them "not relevant to the main theme," or which "conflict chronologically" and so on. The result is that they often perpetuate the circulation of outdated manuals which do not apply under today's circumstances. They remove from study as "peripheral" some of the instrumental materials which were designed not for scholars but for some other purpose, such as to apply a shock or introduce a problem to solve.

Many of these scholars are easily infuriated by students' questions, because the students want to gain some personal insight or advantage which their mentors do not see as the aim of studies in Sufi literature.

What do the students want? Any doubt about the interior method of assessing this should be dispelled when I say that I have only to look over (a) some 150,000 letters received from many countries over fifteen years, and (b) what has transpired in almost innumerable interviews over that time, and (c) press accounts and investigations of the "sufic" cults which have sprung up more or less deliberately in response to a demand for "sufi" knowledge, or which have received fresh life since my publication of *The Sufis* in 1964.

Briefly, the would-be student's head is full of assumptions. I do not mean to say that he should have no preconceptions about Sufism or anything else, but his or her behavior will very frequently show that it is not just a matter of assumptions which may be added to, forgotten or replaced by better facts. The assumptions in the minds of the majority of would-be students in the Sufi field indicate without any doubt not only an underlying desire to join a cult, but a model of what that cult should be like. In other words, the student generally comes to the Sufi in order to have his assumptions reinforced and to join the kind of community or school which, often unknowingly, exists in blueprint in his mind. He may be completely unaware of this. It does not take long to elicit the pattern. I often use a tape-recorder for this purpose. What happens is this.

Instead of asking what he should do and what he should not do, or whether he should do anything at all, the applicant in the course of a conversation wants to know what it will cost him, how much time he will have to spend on it, when the meetings are, where he should live, what kind of job if any he should have, and so on. If he is told "It will take you twenty years," he compares this with the model, and may well ask whether he cannot manage to do it in a shorter time. Finally, by questioning, we find out how much time he will be prepared to give. Similarly, without giving away the reason for the questioning, we find out that he will pay, say, ten dollars a week, but not twenty; he will give three hours a day but not more; he will not read books but will listen to tapes; he will join a group but not study alone; and so on. When this kind of thing happens, I may summarize it all and tell him: "We have determined that you want a community within 35 miles of your place of residence, which will give you solace from your present problems, which has exercises but not prayers, gives you constant encouragement and a great deal of criticism, and which promises power, fulfillment or happiness. You do not need Sufi study, you need such-and-such a cult." There is always a suitable cult, since cults, social groupings, have almost always come into being as a response to needs of this kind.

The foregoing, it will be noted, is a psychological method of determining what someone wants. Its main value is to show when we are not dealing with a would-be student, but a would-be *customer* or client: someone who has a framework and is seeking something to fit it.

So, in cases such as these, our job has merely been to clear away the underbrush. It is my hope that with the growth of mass information about mental models of this kind, we will no longer have to go through this kind of procedure, because it is one which someone, by means of self-questioning, or with the help of a psychologist or even an interested friend, could do for himself, leaving us to get on with the business of working with people who are genuinely interested. To be genuinely interested, of course, means that the person's basic needs (for comfort, repetitiousness, sense of the profound and of being involved in meaningful things, his socio-psychological needs) shall either be stabilized by membership of something which keeps these desires engaged; or else that he is sufficiently autonomous not to need this study as social support therapy.

If you read Sufi writings you will find that much time is given to liberating people from these needs.

Other parts of Sufi literature are addressed to people who no longer have such needs, or who have stabilized them by membership of social entities where these intakes, these nutritions, are supplied. Some people nowadays, it is amusing to note, have seized upon manuals from remote historical times formerly current among Sufis, which effectively supply a social context – a series of maxims and ways of conduct – in order to provide a stable base from which the would-be students could proceed to Sufism. In these days such a thing is not necessary, because the development of so many human organizations of a social, cultural, literary, scientific and other kind provides such formats, and it is only necessary to be integrated into one or more of these to be able to give one's liberated attention to Sufi studies. The most that reliance upon medieval "conduct of dervishes" books can do is to create, as are now coming into plentiful being, new communities admirably suited to the atmosphere of the *thirteenth century* or thereabouts.

Luckily, mostly due to the proliferation of human societies in this era, there are enough well-adjusted people already meshed with their organizations for us to be able to find relatively numerous individuals without having to set up alternative "tribes" or societies. These are the ones to whom our writings and other materials are normally addressed. New research materials are also appearing, relating Sufi tradition to current psychological and social research.

The quasi-Sufi activities of the cultists, and the almost sterile ones of the limited scholars too, have their advantages for us. They hive off numbers of people who would overwhelm us if they were all to apply for Sufi instruction. And they too are satisfied. Both lots believe that they are right, and derive pleasure from this fancy.

The fresh adaptation of Sufi action leading toward the Sufi experience of which I speak, which has attracted so many, and enraged others, is nothing more nor less than successive adaptation of practical activity toward the same end in new circumstances. This is, of course, just the same sort of adaptation which can be seen in Sufi activities in the past, and which accounts for the seeming differences and undoubted variety of ancient Sufi methods, postulates and organizations. Sufi sages throughout the ages have always confused outward students by claiming that all Sufis are essentially one, that all Sufism is the same, whether practiced by means of this technique or that, whether by the Shiahs (e.g., the Bektashis) or Sunnis (e.g., the Qadiris) – nominally and often literally opposed schools within Islam. In the "Table-Talk" of Rumi (d. 1273), entitled *Fihi Ma Fihi*, as in many other places in the literature, we find that many non-Muslims were among those who understood his teaching best. Someone asked Rumi how it was that a whole group of Greek Christians, "unbelievers," could be appropriately affected by his Sufism, when only one Muslim in a thousand could understand it. Rumi explained, with a plenitude of allegories, that externals were not Sufism, and that opinion and dogmas were not the point of it at all. The confusion is in the paths, not in the objective. And, of course, in Aflaki's record of Rumi's work, we have the famous account of how he had disciples of all origins. When he died, multitudes of Christians and others followed his bier. Someone asked one of them why he should weep for a Muslim, and he said: "He is the Moses, the David, the Jesus, of the age. We are his followers, his disciples. This is why we weep."

So here we have Rumi, in the thirteenth century, communicating Sufi understanding to non-Muslims better than he can to "one in a thousand" Muslims. He has dominated the communications gap – not an easy thing to do. It is small wonder that Sufis have again and again come under suspicion by pedestrian minds for this ability, which such minds not only lack, but are generally almost unable even to conceive. So difficult is this problem for superficial thinkers to solve that it is generally held that it was not until al-Ghazzali

(d. 1111) that it was proved, through his work, that Sufism was compatible with Islam and was an inner function of religion itself. Ghazzali is credited with having established the acceptability of Sufism within Islam. Ghazzali, of course, was working for his time, as well as for such succeeding generations as might contain people who would feel the need to question the validity of Sufism. In the Islamic world there are still people who aver that Sufism is not from Islam; or, if it is, that it is not necessary, since the *Qur'an* and the *Traditions of the Prophet* exist. They can only be reassured by the arguments of Ghazzali.

This question of the attunement of the teaching to the culture of the time is most strikingly demonstrated in the work of Ibn Arabi, the Spanish Sufi, known as The Greatest Sheikh, who died in Damascus in 1240. His book *Fusus al-Hikam*, "Facets of Wisdom," takes the teachers as Adam, Seth, Noah, Enoch, Abraham, Isaac, Ishmael, Joseph, Jesus, Solomon, Moses and Muhammad and treats them as concentrators upon various modes of awareness and teaching. The fact that he chooses historical or semi-historical individuals as the focus of his work indicates, of course (among other things), the Sufi awareness of "time, place and people" – the cultural environment, as we would call it today, in certain senses. In this he follows the tradition of Islam, that of the theory of supersession in revelation, which is also acknowledged in other faiths, including Christianity and Judaism, but which is, among Sufis, strongly stressed. Of course, Arabi's work is in many respects addressed to the communities of his day, and its wholesale adoption as a sort of holy writ by sometimes well-meaning but often unregenerate amateurs succeeds only in maintaining an Ibn Arabi cult.

Arabi, in his *Tarjuman al-Ashwaq*, "The Interpreter of Desires," wrote a most remarkable book to show both Sufi truths and the fact that many religious people could not understand religion if it were presented to them in a form to which they were unaccustomed. This is one of the most daring and noteworthy events in public Sufi history. The book reads like a love poem, and Arabi's statement that it was mystical in content was attacked by a theologian who claimed that he probably "adopted this device in order to protect himself from the imputation that he, a man famous for religion and piety, composed poetry in the erotic style." Ibn Arabi himself wrote an explanatory commentary, which was read out in the presence of his critic and other divines. When the critic heard this read, he said "that he would never in future doubt the good faith of any Sufis who should assert that they attached a mystical signification to the words used in ordinary speech," and the use by Sufis of all manner of materials to convey their meanings thenceforward became well-established. Or at least, people could always refer to Arabi's teaching-event to explain why they were working with materials which the devout could not understand.

But a lot of education is still needed. There is at least one contemporary scholar who counts the number of times I myself use the word "God," and judges me on it, so he says; although I might well have doubted this statement from a Western thinker had I not seen it in print, I do confess. No doubt that since I have used the word in some of my books many more times than Arabi in his *Tarjuman*, I can be assessed by such observers as this, as that much more important even than the Greatest Sheikh!

The attunement of the teaching to the facts of "Time, Place and People" is a vital clue in the study of Sufism. It should always be remembered that in Sufi matters there are clearly two forms of study:

1. *ABOUT* SUFISM, which means trying to familiarize oneself with the literature or to concentrate on a form of it, or on concepts and practices which most likely have been tailored for completely different conditions.

2. *IN* SUFISM, which means that the things studied should be those which will enable the student to become a Sufi, which includes the inexpressible Sufi experience.

Sufis study IN Sufism; and matters ABOUT Sufism, if dealt with at all, must involve the minimum of their attention. The reverse is true of externalist scholars. The scholars say that they are objective and the Sufi is subjective. The Sufi says that nobody who does not see the whole picture can be objective, that the person who tries to assume an objective posture is unable to do so until he has had the experiences which alone grant objectivity. From the point of view of the Sufi, the scholar's (and similar) approaches are inadequate. From the viewpoint of the externalist, the Sufi is dealing in capricious things, and is inefficient and inconsistent in saying that he will only teach something which will have an effect, not the whole corpus of materials. Their positions have already been defined and explained, *inter alia*, by Ghazzali, almost 1,000 years ago.

To continue faithful to my claim that we will deal to the greatest possible extent with what will help those who are genuinely interested, rather than with those who have inner reasons for not learning, we must leave the discussion

NEGLECTED ASPECTS OF SUFI STUDY

and information element here, or we would be in danger of becoming argumentative philosophers rather than workers in the field of greater human development. The next part of this exposition will deal with the problems which Sufis find in conveying the truth of their experiences, and how these are solved. We can prepare for this by noting two of them. The first is that when people have an overriding interest, a preoccupation, this may have to be solved before they can study Sufism. Someone, for instance, who says: "Why are Sufis not involved in political action?" is clearly interested in political action and should stick to it until Sufism becomes more interesting to him or her, or until he or she becomes so really dedicated to political action (or anything else) that Sufism is not a real interest any more.

When the mind is full of established biases, it will not be able to graft Sufism on top of them. I will end with the poem of Rumi to this effect, and you will see its equivalence to the way in which things about obsession, conditioning and preconceptions are put in more modern language:

> Two insects eat from the same place
> But from one is a sting and the other honey.
> Both kinds of deer have the same grazing and water –

From one dung, the other musk.
Each of two canes feeds from one thing:
This one is empty: the other full of sugar.

Har do gun zambur khurdand az mahall
Lek shud z'in nish, z'an digar asal.
Har do gun āhu giya khurdand wa āb –
Z'in yaki sargin shud, w'az an mushk nāb.
Har do nai khurdand az yak ābkhūr:
In yaki khali wa az an shakar.

It is not our experience that people in the East can always understand Sufism better than people in the West. At the same time, even in educational circles in the West, the influence of the commercial society perhaps has produced attitudes which inhibit learning capacity, that of Sufism included. The example which has struck me most forcibly is connected with assumptions about what one is to teach, and what ground this is to cover.

I continually receive requests from schools, colleges, universities and learned and social bodies of all kinds, asking for lectures. People want to know about Sufism. In several hundred such cases I have replied saying that I will happily lecture, providing that the audience will first familiarize itself with the basic information about Sufism which is to be obtained from books. I say this because it seems quite absurd to me for a lot of people to collect and to listen to someone repeating something which has been written down and can be assimilated by reading. If people are indeed interested, is it not to be expected that they will be prepared to familiarize themselves with what has been written, and then ask someone to talk to them on more advanced or extra aspects, and also to answer questions based on the fundamental reading? You may be interested to know that, out of these some hundreds of approaches between 1964 and 1974, only one organization ever agreed to ask its audience to do the basic reading.

What does this show? It may show that people want to exercise curiosity (what is this man like?) or that they do not believe that you can get anything from books (though I have written books on the subject, and what were those for?). It cannot be that the students can understand only if *spoken* to, and not through the written word. If that were so, they would probably be so backward that there would be little point in addressing them anyway. Such people exist, too, in the East. But they tend to be found most often among those who have been exposed to Western-style advertising, where the feeling is engendered that something can be obtained or enjoyed by what they imagine to be the "easiest" course, in this case by listening.

What makes this all the more interesting is the nature of the reactions. Some people have become quite annoyed with me for asking them to get to know something of the subject first, as if they were hiring me to do their work for them. In fact, one or two have actually said such things as "Why should our people read when you can tell them?" I am afraid that they become even more annoyed when I ask why anyone should give a talk on, say, beekeeping to people who could not understand words – how far back do we go? Others say, as if it made any difference to the discussion, "The presence of the personality makes all the difference." Difference to what? Basic facts about Sufism do not need a personality to convey them.

Sufism, in education, needs the sort of audience which will be able to attend to what the Sufi and Sufism say.*

The study of Sufism requires a trained observer. In the Western scientific and literary-scholastic traditions, certain minimum capacities

---

* The block, which Sufis call the "veil," which people or human modes of thought interpose between the knowledge and themselves, can effectively mean that at times and in places there is nobody to tell. The *Anwar i Suhaili* puts it thus:
> "Raz makusha ba har kas ki dar in markazi khak Sayr kardim base, mahram israr na bud"
>
> "Do not offer the mystery to everyone, for in this center of earth
>
> We have traveled enough, and there was no helper of the secrets"

are demanded before the observer, student or researcher can be said to be capable of carrying on his investigations. Naturally, these qualifications help in two ways: first, they help to assure others that the observations are likely to be good and sensible, secondly they are the tools which enable the worker to explore his theme and profit from it. In Sufism exactly the same criteria apply. The investigation of Sufism has to be carried out by someone who is himself qualified by having the background which will enable him to research the right phenomena, at the right time, in the right place; enable him to experience what he has encountered, and, ideally, enable him to render this in a communicable form to others. You do not do the watchmaker's job with the bootmaker's tools, and an admirable nuclear physicist may make a very indifferent mechanic or philosopher. Scientific training is needed for scientific investigations. Sufi training is needed for the exploration and understanding of Sufism. This simple fact is obscured by the unconscious assumption that current intellectual and scientific approaches are suitable for all studies; even, perhaps, that they are better than any others; even, perhaps, that the thing being observed cannot itself be assumed to have methods and procedures which have been devised for observing it. We should, however, not be too hasty. Western observers started by looking at outside and backward peoples and histories before they started to analyze themselves with their own tools. Some sort of a hangover of this attitude may be present in the failure to grasp too readily that a thing may already have its own science, and a visible one.

The great poet Hafiz has spoken of the approach by diligent study of the ordinary sort as being impossible – as have so many of the other Sufi masters:

> Qadri majmu'a gul murgh i sahar
>   danad wa bas
> Ki n'ar har waraqi khwanad ma'na danist
> Ai ki az daftar i aql ayat i ishq amuzi
> Tarsam in nuqta be tahqiq nadani danist

> Only the bird perceives the rose totally
> As not everyone who reads a leaf
>   knows its meaning
> O you who from the book of reason
>   would see the signs of love
> I fear that you cannot fathom this
>   subtlety by research

The Sufi study methods involve a preparation of the psychology of the learner's mind by a variety of methods, which must correspond with his or her mental set and the condition of subjective characteristics: the conditioned or immature self which tends to control him, and makes further progress impossible until it has been brought into subjection, set aside or transformed.

Some methods are publicly known, but their devising and application depends upon many factors and is so finely tuned that there is no point in trying to adopt them from books as "devotional exercises" and so on.

"Sufism is studied by means of itself." Some people answer, "But why should I study it in order to find out if it is any use to me?" The answer to this, of course, is simply, "There is no reason why you should do so unless you want to, this desire being based on what you read and what you hear about it." The children of the consumer society are accustomed to asking "Why should I do this or that?," and being told that it is "Because it will make you bigger, calmer, richer, happier, more successful" and so on. And so they frame their questions in this way. And, consequently, by the hard sell or the soft sell, they either buy or refuse to buy. But the Sufi materials are not put in this way at all. On the contrary, we find that it is generally only when people have got over this phase of expecting something greater for themselves that they are able to learn in Sufism.

There is, of course, the so-called third way of dealing with things: discussion. In this, it is held, the purpose is not to buy or to sell a system or idea, but to have it out, work the thing through, by discussion. People insist that if you do not discuss with them, you must be paranoid. This holds good, however, only when we are working in a field where discussion is in fact useful. It is interesting to note that many people who are full of Sufi arguments taken from books and supposedly Sufi circles, have failed to register the many passages in the teaching which say such things as "Someone being saved from drowning does not ask your parentage." It is a matter, as in all educational situations, of what *is* relevant.

Discussion is useful only in matters requiring discussion. It may be of less value when it is only a matter of someone who insists on discussion, needed or otherwise: the *need* to discuss.

An instance comes to mind: admittedly an exaggerated case, but after all it is the more pronounced varieties of diseases which are used for illustration purposes. A man came to see me and said: "If I go to Oxford and get a doctorate of philosophy, I can end up as the head of the BBC. What equivalent can Sufism offer?"

Please note that he had not even registered that there is only one head of the BBC, and plenty of PhDs, and even Oxford DPhils, are nowadays tending hamburger stalls. He was an intelligent man with a good position in life. But as he could only think in terms of the consumer society, and in terms of rank and power and presumably what he imagined might be happiness, I could only say, "Brother, we have nothing whatever to offer you." Now, as far as I can find out, he is quite happy, having concluded that Sufism does not offer anything that he might have been missing.

The possible role of Sufi attitudes in education, particularly in the contemporary world, seems distinctly to be in making clear in such terms as these that we are living in a world where certain orientations – such as those just described – are so common that we don't know that we are their prisoner. Sufis hold that there is all the difference in the world between your ambition commanding you, and you commanding it. I am sure that, now that so many human difficulties have been surmounted, man- and womankind is in a position to give attention to those possibilities of human flexibility which previously had no "cash value" and hence were underdeveloped.

One of the most useful extrapolations from Sufic experiences which are usable on ordinary study levels are what we call teaching-stories. Several hundred of these are now in print in Western languages, assembled from the classics, from oral tradition and also specially written for present-day cultures. Their impact and value has been very extensive. By familiarizing readers with concepts which they had not considered before, the stories have been appreciated as an educational tool in psychology and also in general education. Many, for instance, are in use both for schools and in teacher-training courses. These materials have also been adopted for improving thinking methods and for relating various concepts in a manner which was previously found difficult, or impossible, by various kinds of experts, including workers even in physics.

We have found the stories useful in confirming feelings which people already had but did not know how to relate to thinking patterns.

One actual teaching function of the tales lies in having people select the ones they like, and the ones they understand, and then discarding these, to work for the time being with the remainder. This is, of course, the reverse of the usual method when people tend to concentrate upon what attracts them in any material, including religious materials, and working with that. By making the person attend not just to selected stories or things which impress him most, but upon the whole range of the stories, we are able to prepare areas of his thinking which he would generally neglect. Successive depths and levels in interpretation of the stories signal an increasing development of awareness, and make it possible to understand at once the stage arrived at by the student, and to do the further work with him.

We find that the range and variety of the stories are most useful in dealing with many of the victims of misinformation who have recently started to adopt emotional forms of "Sufism" from books and certain Middle East cultists. Because the stories cover such a range, and because many of them come from such authorities as Ghazzali and Rumi, who are at least notionally accepted by these people, they are able to widen their vision and, often, ultimately to escape from the near-clinical states of excitement and depression in which they have so often spent a great deal of time.

The repertoire of Sufi tales and their content and versatility are almost infinite: Sufi knowledge can be furthered, and traditionally as at present is furthered, by the application of impacts. Here tales and encounters merge. Sometimes this takes the form of introducing incongruities which make the individual think or make his mind work in another, sharper and clearer, fashion. Sometimes it is necessary to redeem the jaded awareness first. This technique, too, can be used, and is employed, in a contemporary context. The most familiar technique is that of jokes. In the Mulla Nasrudin corpus, in addition to the structures which the jokes embrace (which is something else), the "blow" administered by the joke makes possible a transitory condition in which other things can be perceived. The fact, often noted by book reviewers, that many Nasrudin stories are not jokes at all, is also part of the total technique. The intention here is to prevent the stabilization of this form of humor into funny things and those which are not funny. The Nasrudin story is intended to be unexpected.

But what *is* the unexpected? This brings us to a further important consideration of the Sufi attitude toward perceptions, which does cut across quite a lot of customary Western reactions. We are all aware that children like jokes, and they mostly go through a phase when they love the most banal and absurd jokes, and even like to repeat them again and again, almost at times to the verge of hysteria. Then comes the period of cultivation of the sense of humor, when the "mature" – so-called – individual responds only to new, unexpected or subtle jokes. Western observers have often remarked at the childishness of many Eastern peoples, who like to hear puns, like to have old jokes repeated, take pleasure in small incongruities. Punning is the lowest form of humor, by Western standards. Few people – if anyone at all – seem to have bothered to wonder whether the "wearing out" of the impact-capacity of a joke is ennui or maturity; whether it is an advance or a form of insensitivity. The Sufi usage of discontinuities (though you may have to take my word for it here) makes it possible for people to derive as much enjoyment from something which they have seen or heard before, as from something completely new to them. In some active circles it is even a test of ability to understand some advanced concepts, to see whether someone is "too sophisticated" to react to a gentle impulse rather than an ever-different, ever-harsher one. People who cannot do this (as well, let it be said, as having sophistication) may have to undergo a certain kind of sensitivity training before they can reacquire this "childish" capacity. The nearest comparison I can readily find in the West is the fleeting states when people think things are funny or interesting in altered states of awareness brought about as byproducts of drugs, hypnosis, overexertion and so on. In the East there are many examples on record of people repeating poetry or various texts, often very well known ones, including ritual repetitions, and suddenly realizing what they mean, in a sort of inspiration, as though the impulse came from outside.

Ibn Arabi, the great Andalusian teacher, it will have been noticed, speaks of this in what are almost recognizably "modern" terms when he says that knowledge is not gained, it is there all the time. It is the "veils" which have to be dissolved in the mind. He also speaks of God as the name given by man to the impulse which originates all kinds of developments, rendered in customary terms as the deity which most people associate with that word; but nonetheless important by reason of his referring to it in what we would today call scientific terms – and this in the thirteenth century.

The contemporary situation regarding Sufi ideas is worth examining, I think, because we have on this planet, and even within one and the same community, as often as not, very divergent views on whether what has in the past been called mysticism and religion is to be seen in a psychological, scientific or votive light. The battle continues, with the West today still fighting about many points which were, interestingly enough, stated and answered in a most illuminating manner centuries ago in the East. While the present inebriation caused by the descent of every kind of mind upon the Sufi heritage is still raging, and as books strongly tinged (to say the least) with special pleading pour from the presses, there is still much that we can find in the traditional literature to illustrate the equal validity of all three approaches. The special pleaders, as is always the case, will catch up with us in their own good time. Meanwhile they must think as they think, probably because to do so supports their need for reductionist symmetry, even at the cost of truth.

After all, if to them symmetry gained through oversimplification *is* truth, there is nothing that we can do until they have ceased to need such crutches. But they and others imagine them to be spiritual people.

The first requirement for those who wish to know more, no matter the cost to their cherished beliefs is, in the West as in the East, to define where things have gone wrong. The basic error seems undoubtedly to be that while Sufis and others take a working hypothesis to help them guide a student to a certain point, others seize upon what they say and do as being perennially applicable, and mistake such statements for laws or rules. If, for instance, I say, "It is not far to New Jersey," this is a relative statement, produced for a purpose. It cannot be true at all times, in all company, everywhere in the world. Luckily for us today, many Sufis have in the past made a point of asserting this relativity; and therein lies the secret of flexible thought, even the potentiality of progress, since if you believe that something is true, you will not try to think, be or do something which seems to conflict with that "absolute." This may seem elementary. Just apply it to the observation of the lives of people around you, including your own, and to books which you read, and you will soon see how to transcend limitations. I do not here mean that you will necessarily, without other coaching, *be able* to transcend limitations at will, but a theoretical grasp of this will be better than none at all. The rightly mocked phrase "If God had intended us to fly he would have given us wings" is still very much with us in reality, though it now hides behind unexamined assumptions.

A thousand years and more ago, it was being written in the East that "Sufism was formerly a reality without a name; now it is a name without a reality." In the present day, there are plenty of cults and plenty of approaches to Sufism. Some of us are interested in the reality, still, and are not greatly disturbed by the names. This is something of an advance, because it enables us to register that such-and-such a cult or group, whatever its name, is playing out a role which its members need. If it calls itself "Sufi," we do not need to find much harm in that, since the advantage to the members is that they are happy, or happy in their misery, feel fulfilled or feel significance in their struggle for fulfillment.

The information side of what real Sufis are doing is, of course, important, but constitutes only a fraction compared to the total activity. All Sufi endeavors have this iceberg-like reality, and we do take the rendering of Sufic ideas on comprehensible lines, for East and West, seriously. Here is one example:

NEGLECTED ASPECTS OF SUFI STUDY

I was recently approached by people from the BBC in London, to take part in a broadcast about the "effect of Eastern and other anti-intellectual cults, such as astrology, in and on the West." A distinguished Western thinker was saying that the invasion of soothsayers and suchlike was undermining Western culture, and would lead to its serious, if not complete, deterioration. The mentality which was being so deplored was characterized as "Magical" – in the widest sense – "thinking."

When the approach was first made I was away in the Middle East, and my assistant, feeling that this orientation was highly speculative and, however alarming, hardly in line with Western thought itself, let alone my approach toward it, sent some reprint material to the producer who had written, and suggested that the subject should be approached with caution, if at all. His belief, although he said that we might have a meeting to discuss it, was that a sight of the enclosed literature which clearly indicated our stand on the subject, would allow the matter to be decently buried. But things so fell out that I found myself, soon afterward, talking to a highly articulate and well-educated BBC representative.

I explained that first, I did not know of any evidence on which the contention of the magicians and so on doing harm could be based; and second, whoever had said it should, surely, produce such evidence, not just be able to magnetize interest by shouting it out, so to speak. I also pointed out that someone who objected to wholesale imports of Eastern and magical cults should, presumably, be accompanied or opposed on the program not by me but by someone – say a Guru – who thought that they *should* be so imported. I continued that the only other individual that I could visualize as taking part in such a discussion would be someone who might take the middle way and say, as a scientist, for example, that there might be bits and pieces which could be adopted from Eastern or magical lore to the advantage of the West.

I am happy to report that I was able to convey this picture, which included my own incompetence and irrelevancy in such a program. But what surprised me was that there was relatively little interest in, let alone knowledge of, the fact that the alleged situation (cults, anti-cult and taking bits from cults) might very likely not be the true one at all. Furthermore, the assurance that, all over the Western world, there were perhaps millions of people interested in the study of Eastern ideas in a different way from the three alternatives offered, seemed to raise little enthusiasm.

In the East we are used to cults, and in general take little notice of them. The people who appeal to easily conditioned or hysterical followers in the West exist in the East, too, but their clientèle is confined for the most part to certain types in any community, whatever their culture. We have learned to live with these gurus, like you in the West live with hysterical advertising or various fashion crazes. People on the whole do not take them seriously.

But this statement alone, when made in the West, is still often met with amazement or embarrassment. Further, our own efforts to render so-called "Eastern" ideas in terms of Western culture and preoccupations, at least in part, likewise encounter great surprise. And yet there is no doubt in my own mind, and in that of many other people working in this field, that it is this last method of approach and study which is having the greatest real effect and which will have the most permanent importance. The confusion is undoubtedly due to the fact that too many people, in the West, still regard things which are most colorful or make the most noise, as the most significant for their time, their culture, their future. Experience to the contrary does not always teach such people a lesson.

Because in the East we have been exposed to tolerated and widely varying numbers of spiritual teachers for many centuries, the whole institution has been able to settle down. People have even developed a feel for the real functions being exercised by a supposedly spiritual body or teacher, and have been inoculated against the worst likely excesses of charlatans.

As the West continues to develop and attract material from centers of study and all kinds of individuals involved in esoteric matters, far beyond the former confines of the cranks, we may expect a similar development here.

> Pass from names and look at qualities
>   [says Rumi]
> So that the qualities may show the way
>   to the Essence
> The difference of people came about
>   from names
> When the inner meaning [ma'ana] is
>   reached, peace descends.
>
> Dar guzar az nam wa binigar dar sifat
> Ta sifatat rah numayad sue dhat
> Ikhtilaf i khalq az nam uftad
> Chun ba ma'ana raft, aram uftad.

The "names," the external formulations, including labels, are there to enable one to pass from them into reality, into the essence. As soon as the "names," the different external forms, become a matter of comparison, dissension descends. This is why Ibn Arabi says that the teacher must

NEGLECTED ASPECTS OF SUFI STUDY

maintain to his students that his path is the only way. Since, for example, you and I are not comparative topographers but people who, say, want to get from A to B, miscellaneous studies in the various routes and even in whether they are routes at all cannot take place. What has to happen is that someone maintains that he knows the way and that others accept this. This leads to a teaching situation. Rumi puts it even more clearly when he says: traditional knowledge is like using sand to clean yourself when water is available. "Become ignorant and be trusting, to be released from your ignorance."

Sufi study is not a matter of establishing a permanent and unchanging format for following it, but a matter of the existence of people who will be able to maintain the outward flexibility that is rooted in the knowledge of what Sufism is – the knowledge which is an inward experience. As the saying has it, the Sufi teacher's duty is to have what the learner needs, no more and no less. I am also quite sure that, as the general assessment capacity among the public grows through experience, and especially by being exposed to as many real and self-deluded Sufis as possible, including charlatans, there will be the positive gain, right across the board, of identifiability of real Sufis and real teaching, certainly of its expressions through its adaptability and a consequent shriveling of cults and abandonment of easy-answer systems. But we should remember that people will tend to get the "Sufis" they deserve. If there were fewer receivers of stolen goods, there would be fewer thieves. If there were no greedy people there would be no con men. If you want something rewrapped, you will get a difference only in the wrapping.

Once upon a time, it is related, there was a man who had to give a present to someone he did not like but wanted to impress. He found himself in the china department of the great and expensive London departmental store called Harrods and was looking around when there was a sudden crash. Someone had knocked down a costly Eastern vase, and it was soon being swept up in fragments under the eye of the department's manager. Our hero suddenly had an idea. He asked the manager:

"What's going to happen to that – it is going to be mended, I suppose?"

"No, the labor cost would be too great; we are throwing it away."

"I'll give you five pounds for it."

As soon as he was the owner of the shattered vase, the man asked Harrods to pack it and send it by post to the man he had to give the present to.

The idea, as you will have guessed, was that the recipient would think that it had been broken in the mail, but had been worth $1,000.

NEGLECTED ASPECTS OF SUFI STUDY

The vase arrived all right. But when it was unpacked, it did not escape anyone's notice that every single piece had been carefully wrapped in tissue paper by the store's packing department.

Sufi teachings, including exercises and literature, have often been taken apart in the West, broken down and rewrapped, and then delivered to the grateful consumer. The only difference from our story is that most of the students who have done the smashing don't know that they did it; most of the people who did the wrapping thought that it was the right method.

I am constantly coming across examples of this process, which has been going on for a very long time. In my own case, no sooner have I published a book – sometimes only given a lecture – than I find the materials broken down and reassembled and given out as part of existing knowledge (in the case of scholars), or as materials of esoteric importance (in the case of the cultists). And this is not experienced by me alone.

If it is objected that the parallel is not exact, since the recipient could not fail to observe that he wasn't getting a whole vase, let me just say that it is only a matter of time before this part of the story is fulfilled.

We can look at the approach to Sufi perceptions in the light of three stages of learning. This, again, closely follows the right and wrong ways in scientific education and research, though not the pattern of the occult-esoteric attitudes with which Sufism has sometimes been confused:

1. ENJOYMENT: when people learn little, whatever they may imagine they are doing, since emotion fills them and becomes, as it were, something which they are consuming. People in this phase are merely amusing themselves, though they may be good citizens, depending on how they behave. This is rooted in greed.
2. EMPLOYMENT: when people try to use materials prematurely (before they have been sufficiently prepared to attain any real knowledge). This is rooted in impatience and selfishness. How much to try to use is the point here.
3. DEPLOYMENT: when the person is attuned to the extent and way in which he can serve and be served, so that the teaching is really able to take effect, to become active in and through the individual.

In any of these conditions, among the Sufis, the instructor's task is to:

1. Have the necessary experience to know the "destination"; the objective.

2. Have the qualities to assess the individual's case.
3. Have the capacity to monitor, and help to conduct, the learner's progress.

Using this framework, it is possible to see how easily people can "go astray" in an improperly articulated "search for Truth." If they enjoy and care to call it "Holy Joy," or enjoy sacrifice and call it "Sanctified Suffering," they occupy themselves with an intake which is a nutrient only for the appetite – emotional stimulus – which should first have been attenuated. This is not, of course, any argument in favor of being miserable. It means that there must be a balance in the emotional diet and an understanding of one's own subjective, evasive proclivities. When people try to "steal" something, to use it too soon, it is because they have a tendency to want to do so before they have taken it in. This means that they do not in fact have what they think they have, because their desire for acquisition and transmission is stronger than their desire to learn. Since we are living in the "abode of decay," this kind of procedure holds good for many other human activities, and you will find it in non-spiritual areas, generally to their detriment. It can be useful to use such areas when one can find them for observation and self-instruction.

With this kind of tool, and with a careful study of the materials contained in various books and lectures, it is increasingly possible under present-day conditions, for people to observe, if not to enunciate, the interior parallelism of scientific, psychological and religious formulations within the observable part of the Sufi phenomenon. The present restlessness, uncertainty as to the future and even the increase in coercive systems, which, often unwittingly, encourage greater and greater sociological and psychological knowledge, make it, in our experience, more and more possible to establish and maintain the kind of community (in the wider sense) in which Sufic study can develop. Where people no longer have certainties linked to coarser material things, they will seek personal and group stabilization by adding some subtler range. Traditionally under these circumstances, they have tended to reach out for this range "beyond." Though we must pay some local prices, some tolls, we have very little to complain about so far as real Sufi prospects in the modern world are concerned.

As with any fresh interest without deep traditional and culture-based roots in a given civilization, there is *bound* to be an overabundance of unsuitable people attracted. Let them be attracted; the study sorts them out. This is true, both in the attraction and in the sorting out, in the branches of science now looking at the Sufi heritage and activity.

Subhani says:

> Are! Alam khiyal ast wali
> Paiwasta dar u haqiqa'i jalwagar ast

> Yes! The world is illusion. But
> (Connected in it), certainty is
>   manifested in it

The Sufis aim at an understanding which can readily be stated as finding other ways of perceiving the world and a knowledge of things beyond the normal ken, which also requires (for it to become effective in our ordinary human sphere) to be assessed and evaluated by intellectual capacities which are not ordinarily found in mechanical thought. Many striking illustrations of this are to be found in the vast repertoire of instruction tales which we call teaching stories and several hundred of which I have published in over a dozen books now in currency both in educational and general use.

Another way of referring to the Sufic development is to say that experiences and perceptions beyond the familiar range are to be gained through what are known as mystical methodologies, but that these can be understood and employed in the mundane situation only when there is a developed means to do so which has been correctly organized in the human mind. So Sufism requires both experience and organization, both perception and interpretation. This distinction, you will observe, is not widely adopted in other systems. A Sufi should be able not only to know, but to do; not only to think, but to have something exceptional to think about.

This Sufic understanding must, because of the foregoing necessities, be developed without any exclusive or out-of-kilter usage of the cultic or the academic approaches, but must employ the advantages of what underlies both. Just remember, if you will, as soon as you see or hear the word SUFI, what associations it conjures up; and match these with what was said by al-Hujwiri in the very oldest Persian treatise on Sufism, *The Revelation of the Veiled*, on the whole subject: "Sufism was formerly a reality without a name; today it is a name without a reality." And it was possible to aver this centuries *before* many of the great Sufi classics and textbooks were written by such great authorities as Ibn al-Arabi of Spain, al-Ghazzali of Persia, Rumi of what is now Afghanistan....

If the object of Sufism is to become a Sufi, to reach a certain kind of understanding of things, which I might call extra-dimensional cognition, and if the goal has been reached and the way to retrace this path is known to living people, and if some at least of these living people are engaged, though not necessarily exclusively, in enabling others to tread this path, certain differences between Sufi thought and action on the one hand, and other more familiar systems on the other, immediately become apparent. Perhaps the most noteworthy of these differences is that the development and applications of Sufism as a study will be organized and projected by the Sufi exponent (a) in the light of his own experience rather than by means of repetitious doctrine; (b) in accordance with the actual potential of his students and not by speaking into a void, as it were; and (c) adapted to prevailing circumstances without cleaving to tradition for its own sake. If the conventional type of teaching organization has a stock of information and tested methods and students of a certain capacity, it will seek to bring these factors together in ways familiar to all of us in the more usual sort of school, university and so on. But, for the Sufi, the world is not at all static, the knowledge to be imparted is seldom formal or factual, the student is neither a pitcher to be filled nor something to be processed, or even regarded as only someone who can learn a skill or is to practice the "profession" of Sufi. The Sufi's position, rather, is that he is someone who has experienced something, who sees how to impart it almost from moment to moment. He structures his method, almost instinctively, so as to help to achieve the desired end. This formulation constitutes the only development and application in which he is interested – indeed, in which he is competent.

To convey this sense of Sufi thought and action is in itself one of the major concerns of the Sufi exponent. In diluted but approximate terms, if the formal, the conventional, thinker says, as has often been stated, "Instruction is information, training and the development of abilities in the student," the Sufi says, "We help to impart Sufi capacity, whether or not this involves instruction, information, training and development. Our role is not to impress or mystify, or to insist on certain acts or beliefs, or even on the reaching of easily quantifiable goals, or yet even to make sure that certain ideals are maintained. What we say and what we do is always subordinate to, and commanded by, our perception of what the learner needs at any given time or place, and under the prevailing circumstances, in order to arrive at similar perceptions." Many people do not want Sufi experiences, whatever they may think or say. It is no part of our task to disturb their real situation.

And so we have the famous saying in a celebrated poem by the thirteenth century teacher Rumi that

NEGLECTED ASPECTS OF SUFI STUDY

the Sufi is "made wise by the Truth," for he is not "a scholar from a book." The book, for the Sufi, is something which fills an instrumental, not an informational or mental exercise role.

Failure to observe the secondary, what I have called lower-level stabilization of the study and action of Sufism, as "water finding its own level," is the direct (and, to the Sufi, as probably to the anthropologist, plainly observable) cause of the theologized, formalistic, mechanical and quasi-academic versions of so-called Sufism in both the East and West. This is most easily demonstrated in the work of orientalist, religiously didactic and ecstasy-oriented individuals and groups whom the late twentieth-century upsurge of interest in our subject has stirred into a frenzy of propaganda and publication; not to mention the also secondary but understandable phenomenon of vituperation directed at those who try to redirect attention to the customary approach which, after all, is abundantly documented in a large number of the extant Sufi classics, upon which both scholarly – derivative – research and "dervish exercises" – mimetic behavior – are allegedly, but in the event highly selectively, based.

But if by Sufi definition (and surely we must listen to it) the real development of Sufism and its applications is not to be found in academic work or in random or uninstructed experimentation;

and if Sufism is to be absorbed by such a judicious process as might be comparable to the working with a master of an art rather than a profession, what of the other widespread and – to some – quite attractive alternative? After all, there are in the West and always have been in the East large and small groups of people and plenty of vociferous individuals as well, who maintain that Sufism, being grounded in experience, and not being available through static scholasticism or automatistic piety, should and must be cultivated by means of overrunning the emotions, by listening to or playing music, by dancing and wearing strange clothes, by changing one's name, and by slavishly following what the participants imagine to be the literal instructions of some preferably ancient and revered but long-dead teacher. Such people, in the nature of things, have far greater social visibility than the often much more inhibited scholars: they and their works are to be found in a larger and much more animated constituency. Because of this, many ordinary people lump them together with all the other cultists, members of esotericist groupings with dauntingly formidable names and even greater pretensions. They call them "nuts" and politely avoid them. I, for one, would not blame anyone for concluding that they are dealing with just another yogic, Hindu, Zen or similar group. Perhaps, though, they are not

NEGLECTED ASPECTS OF SUFI STUDY

strictly similar. But it is equally true to say that such coteries are not Sufi ones in the sense that "Sufi" is employed by the traditional teachers or by contemporary Sufis who maintain a wider tradition and more comprehensive approach. Their activities, indeed, whether emphasizing the playing or hearing of music, or dance, or singing, or recitations, or wearing non-current dress or assuming locally peculiar names, these are all familiar to us in the East and are clearly distinguished in the historical perspective of the Sufi classics as, frankly, deviant forms stabilized on quite obvious social needs. But that which human-sciences people politely call "needs," we often describe more pungently. My purpose in mentioning them is to ask you not to throw the baby away with the bathwater, not to shun Sufism because of them, and not to imagine that there was any useful purpose beyond entertainment to be served by taking notice of them. Remember, they have been with us for centuries and people in most eastern countries where they are to be found have basic, descriptive names for them. And not always very complimentary ones at that.

Both the overly academic and the cultic forms of so-called Sufism, then, might by some, perhaps admissible, stretch of the language be called studies *of* Sufism, but they cannot ever be called studies *in* Sufism.

So there are the usual reactions, seen from one perspective. But what is the brief theory of Sufism? Who are the past and present authorities? What are the standard books? How is it organized? What does it promise, how long will it take, what do I pay and how soon can I join? These are the main questions which I have collected from some tens of thousands of letters from people who, of course, know next to nothing of the subject. I have over 140,000 letters on file, and have in the past discussed this matter with some 20,000 people, though I avoid it as much as possible. Still, about 20 a week is the average of conversations....

The questions may show, I think you will agree, things other than a straightforward search for information and truth. They indicate, for instance, that the questioners are trained in approaching a subject in a certain manner, and that does not include asking "What can you tell me about this subject, including whether it falls into my categories or not?" They seldom, if ever, say "What do I need to know, or how do I have to be, to approach this subject?"

Our experience shows that people who approach matters in the realistic but mechanical manner are not likely to be interested in Sufism at all. The way they approach things shows what they are expecting to meet. They are the servants of a mental model, seeking not knowledge but the fulfillment of expectations.

I say "are not likely" to be interested in Sufism, because the degree of inflexibility which accompanies the so-called systematic approach will vary. I will now ask you to monitor your own reactions when I answer the questions we quoted a moment ago in a manner designed to further Sufi knowledge, not as a mechanical scholar:

There is no brief theory of Sufism. Virtually every single one of the past and present "authorities" has been challenged by non-Sufis as not being a Sufi at all, or not being a "classical" Sufi, or with some other such reproach. There are no truly standard books in the conventional sense, because Sufi books are designed, like Sufi practices, to fit in with local and temporal circumstances, which is why they differ and vary so much. The object of Sufism is to be a nutrient, not to provide entertainment. It does not promise anything, it has no study timescale as in intellectual exercise or social groups, it has and has not got systems of praying (and understands this in various ways), and strictly speaking one does not "join" to become a Sufi.

There is not even a name of universal application for the student or the activity. The "Sufi" is the product of Sufism, which is itself a Western word invented in 1821 by the German scholar Frederick August Thöluck, of Berlin.

And yet all Sufis can recognize one another, though imitators have to rely on signs and signals. This former sensitivity, however, happens through perception of the inner quality, and never depends on outward criteria. If you read a fair cross-section of the books on Sufis and Sufism on the market today (and it is a good market) you will find that various mystical masters and scholars (whom I call the gurus and academics) adduce evidence from books to show that Sufis are only *Muslims*, but also that they are *opposed* to Islam; that they are *Shiahs* of Islam, or that they are only *Sunnis* (these being the two main schools of law among the Muslims); that they originated in *Persia*, in *Greece* or *India*; that they *use* music or condemn it, and so on. All these contentions, of course, and numerous others, reflect only the superficialities which result from looking at *some* of the evidence, or else from trying to amalgamate it all, without realizing that Sufis regard things of the world, of the social and psychological domain, as instruments and will use almost anything which connects appropriately with the attainment of their goal. So we are still at the condition, in externalist studies of Sufism, equivalent to that of the blind men and the elephant, when each blind man seized a part of an elephant and insisted that it was a fan (the ear), a rope (the tail), a pillar (a leg) and so on. This situation is only to be expected, given the circumstances and biases of the people who are working with the residual materials. The same thing – the Blind Men and the Elephant syndrome – would happen if a number of people with various backgrounds and biases were to be let loose on a newly discovered civilization whose bases were unknown to them. Each would try to relate it to a personal or culture-based mental model. In most current forms of investigative culture, too, each would regard the materials found as basic and essential. They would tend not to believe that there might be an inward unity, a deeper level at which the design could be understood.

This situation is not confined to the West or to our time, although it is very marked with us at the moment, so much so that for many people it is the sole reality, rather like life seen on a TV screen might be for someone born and brought up in a sitting-room of the suburbs, and never leaving it.

I would like to make it clear at this point, however, that this attitude is by no means unanimous, and that we have little real difficulty in conveying our way of thinking and our priorities of attitude to a sufficiently large number, though not perhaps a major proportion, of people. The interesting thing to note here seems to me to be that these people are found only in relatively small numbers in the old-fashioned parts of the academic and cultic communities. They are more numerous almost everywhere else. This observation appears to indicate that the activity of the "search for truth," as expressed through scholarly or theology-centered approaches, is in itself a form of employment, a stabilization, which in itself yields satisfactions which prevent any more versatile interest being expressed. By this I mean that these are not so much paths to knowledge as small or large tribes or communities which have an unwitting vested interest in maintaining their methods of thought and action because these give them outlets or satisfactions. The search for truth is, therefore, in such cases, subordinate to the stimuli which come from remaining in a system called "the scientific method" or "exercising the sovereign human intellect," or "the true spirituality which comes through constant ritualistic practice." And who would blame them? I do not feel it necessary to criticize this approach in an unqualified way, though I do think it important, for the sake of other types of people, that an alternative formulation be represented and maintained. I have therefore concentrated, for the most part, on publishing books which further this objective. I am sure that it is the use of one's metier as a personal psychological stabilizer that causes so many observers to try to pluck out just one or two aspects of Sufism to study or try to employ.

NEGLECTED ASPECTS OF SUFI STUDY

Such people use what they call Sufism as an occupational therapy, not to yield its true content.

This is not to say that Sufism is claimed to be *sui generis*, of a unique kind. Such a contention is needed only if we are trying to assert its indispensability or preeminence in some sense. Sufism is, however, something which Sufis themselves always claim is studied by means of itself, by its own tools, and is not susceptible to outward analysis. We have seen, and you can check this in a hundred ways from published literature of all kinds, what happens when people attempt to get to the bottom of Sufism through its "outward forms." People become fascinated by the ESP characteristics sometimes observed in Sufis. But the first requirement in a Sufi student is that he *conceal* this development from outside inquisitiveness. ESP is a byproduct of the process of transcending boundaries.

Sufi literature, exercises, contentions and so on are not ever to be regarded primarily as informational or illustrative. They are instructional, and that is that. Some Sufi materials may have cultural attractiveness, some may contain information, but these are not their chief purposes. When therefore we speak of the "development and applications of Sufism" – these other categories are to be understood to be spin-offs, even at their highest ordinarily visible function. This does not mean that a Sufi who saves someone's life or is active or successful in the quantifiable sense would rather not do it; or that Sufis want to keep materials secret and deplore the imitators' caperings when they mime Sufi specializations. It means that however much the products of Sufi development are valued by non-Sufis, and are contributing to the advance of ordinary knowledge and the tranquillity, progress and success of society, this is a secondary phenomenon to the Sufi. If, by enlarged knowledge, a Sufi does something which other people applaud or think heroic, say, he cannot think of himself as distinguished or a hero, since he has almost by definition a panoramic view of life which has told him both what might happen under certain circumstances and how little ultimate importance this holds (or how much); things which are not understood by those who therefore judge in a local and parochial way. He may even be blamed for not sharing knowledge or for arbitrary action when he and his congeners know that the Sufi role is not capable of exposition.

So the Sufi cannot supply systems and ideas which are designed to be used by a society to improve itself, and for this to be presented as an objective of Sufism. The objective of Sufism is to become a Sufi, and this development, in turn, has an effect, sometimes a determining effect, on individual and group psychology and on society. It is not the other way about. For this reason there are severe limits to the extent to which a Sufi can cooperate in the supply of and in applying things for, as it were, secondary use. The Sufi, "in the world but not of it," will fulfill whatever temporal functions he can, but his task is not in harmonizing with society at all other costs. The fact that Sufis have been able to contribute so much, and continue to do so, to world culture in so many aspects, is not because of just deciding to love man, but because their Sufic experience shows them that human service is necessary; but they have their own perspective on how and when and where it may be most effectively carried out. They are not idealists, who almost by definition have a restricted view, and only hope. It is idealists alone who qualify for the title of "hero."

This statement was being made by one prominent Sufi once, when an interrupter called out: "Then why is the world in such a mess?" Before he could answer another voice shouted: "If it was not for them we would all have been destroyed!" I find this, among other things, an interesting example of the only two ways of thinking (either-or) illustrated by the two main types: the first we may call the intellectual, the other the emotional. Sufi understanding, according to the practitioners, transcends these two modes, valuable though they are for so many purposes. Without them, of course, we would have to cease to be Sufis, and attend to the more basic intellectual and emotional modes on which society is at present stabilized. But that is an area of hypothetical discussion.

We are talking about a "Framework for New Knowledge." This seems to me to imply that there is an interest on the part of non-Sufis to know what new knowledge there is and what the framework might be. But a Sufi will always say that your definition of new knowledge may not be his – or his may not be yours.

We are here dealing with the phase and formulations of the human insight known as Sufism, but now I will try to indicate the Sufi's explanation of the course which the organizing of this path takes in virtually all human communities with similar institutions and expectations.

For the purpose of illustration, we have to start somewhere, and I will start with the man or woman whom the Sufis call Insan al-Kamil (Insani Kamil), which means the Completed Human, though for some reason it is almost always translated into English and other Western languages as the Perfect Man. This realized individual, according to many Sufi authorities, is relieved of the constricting performance of various kinds of social behavior which were intended to help lead to realization. The position is roughly similar to that which obtains in etiquette. This has led to the Sufis being called heretics and apostates, and to the appearance of some large but untypical communities called *Bi-Shara'* (Lawless), and even to the distinction between the *Bi-Shara'* and the *Ba-Shara'* – those who observe the Law. Many Sufis in Islamic countries, including some of the greatest ones, like Hallaj 1,000 years ago, and Rumi, who died in 1273, have said and written things which, in Islamic Law, brand them as apostates. Ibn Arabi and other great teachers of the Sufis have said that a realized Sufi, exempted from repetitious observances because of his attainment will, according to social circumstances, maintain their outward observance for the public good, or will be exonerated by legal decision (as often happened and still does), since it has been upheld by jurists that things said or done or not done in states different from customary consciousness cannot be judged by ordinary criteria. Islamic opinion legitimized the Sufis by means of this formula, almost 1,000 years ago.

So here we have this realized individual, perhaps behaving in an inexplicable, or at any rate, an often misunderstood manner. He may be put to death, as many were, including Hallaj in the tenth century, when bigotry overcame justice. He may acquire a great reputation. If this happens, people may seek to emulate him, primitively thinking that, for instance, the induction of the ecstatic experience of itself produces self-realization. Some of these imitators will be sincere, others will attempt to pretend to be mystics and Sufis. Both types may attract followers and, through deceit or faulty understanding, may establish "schools" and communities which, modern Western knowledge verifies, are most logically to be assessed as at best social groupings, whose participants not only claim and believe that theirs is a legitimate spiritual endeavor but have in a sense (a very restricted sense) a right to do so. If, after all, your sense of religion or higher things is at a level at which, say, circling around a totem makes everyone taking part quite certain that they are psychically elevated, this is indeed a religious and "higher" activity within the local definition, and that is that. Religion exists at many levels, as the Sufi classical tale of Moses and the shepherd pungently reminds us.

But I would not like to say that either the imitation or the well-meant consolidation of a community forms a "Framework for Knowledge," new or otherwise. The next stage is when what, for lack of a better term, we might call an illuminate, having experienced the state of integration or "completeness," and having been able to discern what restrains ordinary people from reaching it, constructs a teaching method designed to facilitate arrival at this state. Such people are those who are known as Sufi teachers. The technical terms most often used for the wise or realized ones are Sheikh (Arabic) and Pir (Persian), both denoting in this usage something like "Elder." The teacher is known, in all Sufi circles, as a Murshid, director. The status of both Pir (Elder) and Murshid (Director) may be the same, but not all Elders are Directors, Teachers and conductors of the Way.

The Director establishes his rule. Historically, this rule is easily seen to coincide with the social situation and mentality of the people among whom the Teacher works and is authoritatively described as such, as by Arabi in the West and Hafiz in the East, in Iran. His community need not be concentrated in one place, or use ecstatogenic methods, or even have regular or frequent meetings. His basic watchwords include "Speak to everyone in accordance with his understanding," and "The phenomenal is the Bridge to the Real." Such teachers may or may not be publicly known, and may have very few students, and from time to time none at all.

The vast number of types of allegedly Sufi schools, and the seeming differences between their observances, are due to two factors. The first is that each teacher may establish a separate "rule" or system, which corresponds with both his own individuality and the surrounding facts of his time and place. The second is when this director is dead, and the participants in what he had established as an ongoing and flexible rule, feel the need of stabilization or, rather, the desire for it, with the removal of the teacher as its center of gravity.

This latter stabilization is often the adoption of specific exercises, formerly used in a limited way, as technical instruments under special circumstances, as the new binding force. Tools have become chains. Everyone now does these exercises, and a near-indissoluble vortex is formed. We now have a cult, not a school.

Anthropologists, sociologists, historians and other specialists, as well as reasonably well-informed lay people, will recognize the pattern. The highly organized phase will either succeed the central figure, or will have been adopted from his initial procedures, and probably constitute the low-level application of discipline or grouping which takes place at the outset of the "teaching course." This deterioration, which has great survival value, might be likened to laboratory assistants maintaining "chemistry" on a do-it-yourself basis by repeatedly washing test-tubes.... Few people realize, though the historical evidence is freely available, that none of the organization of the so-called Sufi orders can be traced to their putative founders, themselves undeniably major teachers.

Many of the followers who succeed Sufi teachers tend to be people who, lacking the personality requirements which mark a "leader," find (consciously or otherwise) that they can stabilize the group by systematic ideas (intellectuality) or action and experience (emotion-based) behavior. Such systematization, which always includes a great deal of telescoping and simplistic formulation, helps to ensure the longer life of the group – it no longer is in great danger of dying with the leader, the leader, here, already being an *imitator* of the founder. But, as Sufis have observed in this connection, "the essential element had died with the teacher." An Urdu proverb underlines the need to remember the objective, not the appearance: *Chalti ka Chizka nam, Ghari hai* (that which *moves* may be called a cart).

This is not to say that the residues of the teaching, the formulae and procedures, the literature and the sayings of the teachers and so on, are of no use. But it does mean that, as with the cargo-cult, even those who have seen, and to an extent taken part in a thing, may be wildly at sea when it comes to keeping its inner reality going. The Sufis tend not to worry too much about this; those who need social satisfactions from something will not be prevented from getting them. For the rest, the phrase "The Secret Preserves Itself" is enough. In organic life, a nutrient becomes a compost and continues life as a fertilizer. In the eyes of the Sufis, literature, for instance, which has not taken effect as a nutrient, conducing to the learning, is admired instead, and thus functions as "compost." I might here add a further reason for the proliferation of imitation Sufi cults. People want to be loved, and we don't always *seem* to love them. We sort out the real learners from the would-be consumers and in the process become great innovators. If the Russians say that Popov invented radio, well – we invented aversion-therapy; this is the best way to get rid of the superficialists.

So the "Framework" is local to the culture, limited to the time, tailored for the people. The recognition by some of the greatest Sufis of the relationship between all mystical experience, irrespective of its religious coloring, is one of the things which many people have been unable to stomach. Most people, however, who have been prepared to give time and effort to understanding this seeming paradox have indeed been able to do so, unless they have psychological "needs" which prevent it. I cannot improve on the material on this subject which has been left by Rumi, Shabistari, Hujwiri and Ibn Arabi – and many others; indeed, I have quoted it extensively in several books, which are very widely bought and studied. I think that it is enough to say that their arguments having prevailed in what was often a far more oppressive and less well-informed atmosphere than we have today, still hold good and need only be invoked.

In the largely Western-oriented culture which covers so much of the world today, I find a problem in the multiplicity of interests and opinions which cause people to take an interest in Sufism. People have, it is true, discovered with surprise that Sufi texts contain materials which they thought were modern scientific discoveries. This only has to be said for its attraction to become instantly apparent. Some people have tried everything else, and we are in a period when through sheer novelty value, Sufism has an attraction for a lot of people. The puerile nature of many Eastern cults as nowadays practiced, has also driven some Western thinkers to Sufism. They should remember that cultic forms of Sufism are not the real study. Some people, following the contemporary idea of "the expansion of human consciousness," feel that if they look into this phenomenon in our terms they may find clues or methods which might enable them to increase perceptions beyond the limitations which they have decided to be undesirable to them.

I remember Robert Graves annoying a lot of dons at Oxford when, elected Professor of Poetry there, he said: "You may not be able to get much out of me. Although I am a poet, a fish is not always the best authority on fish." "But," objected one of the scholars, "you are the greatest poet of the English language!" "Be that as it may," said Robert, "but I can only teach you if your interest in poetry is of the *same kind* as mine." Some of the people there knew what he meant, but others asked for "further definitions" and there were mutterings of "hairsplitting."

Sufis have always maintained that only Sufis understand other Sufis fully, and also that the initial or low-level study of Sufism may be motivated by unSufic ambitions. They may – and do, often heartily – respect the approaches and contributions of good scholars. But I am quite sure, and in this I do not differ from Sufi tradition, that just as science is carried out by its own methods and with its own tools, so is Sufism; that just as intellect gives help in approaching what *it* can understand, and emotion has *its* role, so does the would-be student of Sufism have to be prepared for this study. Sufism cannot be assessed or analyzed or partially used to get to the bottom of it, though its byproducts are socially and psychologically more than just useful. The reason why you cannot penetrate to the core of Sufism and work backwards is that, as it were, this has already been tried and the Sufis' methods and "being" are such that, to borrow words from another level, the research has already all been done. The other day a contemporary Sufi referred to this question with the words: "If you want to reinvent the wheel, no engineer will help you. If you want to study applications of engineering, he may be able to help you. But only if you are talking the same language. It is the same with Sufis." He quoted the Persian phrase for this: "āzmuda rā āzmudan jahl ast" – "to seek to test the tested is ignorance."

The Sufi Abu Said and the philosopher Ibn Sina, known to the West as Avicenna, once met. When they parted, the Sufi said:

> "What I see, he knows."
> The philosopher said: "What I know,
>   he sees."

If you take this to mean that philosophy, which includes the scientific and intellectual attitudes, can arrive at the knowledge which the Sufi is said to have, you will not be at variance with some Sufi authorities who have said that some of the things that Sufis know are arrived at by thinkers, in the end; and certainly many thinkers have been surprised at how many things about the products of intellectual work Sufis have known. But you should note two points here, and noting them is the sort of exercise which one may often find in a Sufi school:

1. The quotation about the Sufi and the philosopher does not say that each knows *everything* that the other "knows" (calls knowledge);
2. The philosopher arrived at his knowledge through the *pursuit of philosophy*, not by the analysis of Sufis and Sufism. The scholar must stick to his methods and his assumptions, and get what he can through them.

It is probably because a Sufi can *only* instruct in Sufism, and because *only* a Sufi can instruct in Sufism, that so many scholars have made what must have seemed to their associates at times the ultimate sacrifice in pursuit of knowledge – like the great theologian al-Ghazzali, they have become Sufis. So far, however, for some reason which you may care to consider, we still have no record of any Sufi who has become, instead, a scholar.

Sufism, in striving to establish and maintain its own teaching system, is often regarded as being in opposition to tested and useful learning procedures, especially in declining to reveal reasonably requested information for no easily understood, much less generally accepted, reason. Why is this?

NEGLECTED ASPECTS OF SUFI STUDY

All cultures assume, until something to the contrary is established, that it is possible to learn anything which has to be learned by the methods which are current in those cultures. This tendency ranges from the New Guinea method of applying sympathetic (imitative) magic in making cargo ship models to get "cargo" from the West; to the contemporary Western habit of trying to learn "Eastern" systems of thought by breaking them down and swallowing a piece at a time in a linear fashion; to the attempts I have seen among some orientals to learn the beauties of literature, including Shakespeare, by committing it to memory and reciting it in a monotone....

Thus, any attempt to state that there are special ways of learning which are not known to your audience is often interpreted by such an audience as a challenge. It challenges their customary patterns.

The responses to a "challenge" of this kind include (a) rejection; (b) indifference; (c) depression, and an anxiety to "change" completely to get into the new and putatively superior pattern.

For the moment we may ignore the first two responses, and can discuss the third.

In our tradition, when we are dealing with the increasing of human capacity, we do not deal in instant conversion, in imitation, in linear thought or in gobbets of attractive information. Still less can we, any more than any other true teaching organization, deal in the induction or assuaging of anxiety, though the latter is standard procedure for cults. Least of all do we deal in emotional vagueness or plunging into ecstatogenic processes.

We do not expect people to abandon their conditioning or their customary ways of doing things. How, then, do we facilitate the means to learn while not disturbing the usual patterns? In just the same way that people teach anything that you cannot do already: we help to teach you something, as a skill is taught, which continues side by side with the existing behavior patterns. While it may be said that in some senses, nobody who learns something is ever exactly the same afterward, this doesn't mean that you have to become, as it were, someone or something else to study Sufism.

It is the Sufi task to *give* you the means to exercise new and superior functions. While you are acquiring such capacities, you must, as does any learner in any other field, continue to live a normal life and be a normal person.... Normal here means to be a member of your social reference-group.

If, as an analogy, you were a baker and learning to become a candlestick-maker, you would continue your baking and practice, in your available time, candlestick-making. You would, of course, not try to make candlesticks with the skills and materials used in baking, except for employing a few correspondences, like the capacity to coordinate.

Al-Ghazzali, the Persian, in his *Alchemy of Happiness*, tells how a scavenger collapsed from the unfamiliarity of the scent when he was walking in the Street of the Perfumers; and how it took a former scavenger to discern his state and its remedy so that he could apply the indicated procedure of holding something filthy under the scavenger's nose until he revived.

Like that scavenger, people in the ordinary world become bemused and ineffective if they are exposed to things from another dimension. They are brought back to "reality" by returning to customary patterns. If the scavenger wants to become, say, a perfumer, he has to be exposed by degrees to sweet odors. At some point he will be able to operate in both "worlds," having learned through practice how to discern both "smells."

The "challenge" to the scavenger was the blast of unadulterated perfume from the perfume sellers' shops. The scavenger had not had the opportunity of being exposed to perfume in the right quantity, quality and other circumstances; he had, therefore, in fact, been "assailed" by the perfume. And he collapsed. Like many people faced by the straightforward claims of esotericists, he might have become bemused, anxious – even desperate to shun garbage collecting to become a perfumer or perfumed person himself. But could he have done it only in the time, at the place, and in the way that he himself demanded? Certainly not.

Anxiety or impatience are similar to feelings experienced in any situation where people have themselves made random assumptions about how much time they need to do something, or how little time they may have left in which to achieve something. It is they, in such a case, and not the school or other source of expertise, which is saying what the curriculum should be. Does such a back-to-front situation not surprise you, when you look at it straight?

The reading of selected passages from books, including Sufi books, those which for example stress questions of haste and urgency, originally addressed to people in specific places, at special times, for appropriate purposes – this is no way to learn about one's own situation. Yet the fault frequently lies in the learner who is not seldom inefficient, greedy or inadequately prepared. He is not listening to the teacher, or not looking at the whole of the picture. If he was, he would find that patience is spoken of as tellingly as urgency. What kind of a cook, say, would develop if someone were to read cookery books but only took heed of the passages which mentioned vanilla or fat or even soups? We must note here that a lot of, as it were, "good potential cooks" don't misinterpret our books at all....

Equally important, *of course*, is the need for the teachers to make this plain, if they are dealing with such backward learners as those who might address themselves to this particular subject in such a bizarre manner. But the teacher is not under any obligation to persist in demanding a change to normality in his students if they will not, or cannot, give him or his materials the kind of attention which they already give to every other subject which they study.

Effectively, though not necessarily in appearance, those with psychological blocks to entering Sufism are not students at all. If there is to be a transaction or a contract between the two parties, both sides must keep to it.

Certain pitfalls in the way of the student who wants to apply himself to Sufi matters can be noted, though I have never seen them summarized or even isolated in print – and this in spite of the fact that at the last count it was found that over the past 50 years in the major Western countries, one book or monograph on Sufism has appeared on an average of *every fourteen days!* So I am condensing three common reactions to Sufi materials, and then jumping rapidly ahead, as a final statement, to the ultimate situation of those who *have*, in fact, learned:

There is a Sufi principle, Al Mujazu Qantarat al-Haqiqa: "the phenomenal is the channel to the *real*," as I mentioned earlier.

Sufi teaching is effected through imposed or calculated experience, and training about how to benefit from experience. People are subjected to written materials, in a literary phase of Sufi activity, which are designed to "strike" them in such a way as to allow the mind to work in a new or different manner. Sufi circles, their members carrying on all manner of (often seemingly mundane or irrelevant) tasks, are settings for seeking the imposition and tasting of experience. The words, the actions – even the inaction – of teachers are a further form of impact teaching. The content of Sufi literature and contact also enable the student to obtain impacts suitable to his state from what are, to others, simply some of the ordinary events of the conventional world. He can see them differently and profit from them more extensively, while still retaining his ability to cope with events in the ordinary world on its customary, more limited, levels.

Because the foregoing is generally not properly understood, there are three, not one, usual reactions to Sufi offered experience to be found:

1. The individual becomes a wiseacre. Instead of profiting from the Sufi impact, he learns

how to "deal with it," answering back, as it were, to frustrate the impact.
2. He becomes hopelessly indoctrinated, obsessional, a "believer" in Sufism who is nothing other than a sensationalist.
3. He (or she) *is* able to observe and to feel the special function of the Sufi impact, on himself, on his fellows, in literature and in other areas. He can detect, and profit from, this activity in many different ways, without being imprisoned by method or associations.

It is this last response which, for the Sufi teacher, signals the emergence of the learning function, the enlightenment, without which no further progress is made. It is at this stage that the student can at last "make sense" of all that has gone before, can profit from his past efforts. If he can anticipate that this is the true sequence of events, he will, even before he reaches it, gain the confidence and stability to continue without constantly trying to "get paid as he goes along." In all other systems, there is an anxiety to cash in, to get something, to feel, to know, to be, to experience, to attain certitude – this is what we call getting paid as you go along. With the Sufi, you do not, however, get paid twice. There is a choice open to all: choose the Sufi opportunity if it comes your way, but at the expense of using it as a source of emotional stimulus. Alternatively, choose a system which promises thrills, chills and spills, stimuli as you go along – and find nothing else. It is the understandable clamor for instant or constant stimuli from the consumer which has brought into being those allegedly Sufi but really concocted systems which offer the emotional junkie "Sufism plus kicks."

Long studies are sometimes needed before the seeker becomes a Sufi. But if Sufi teaching systems are generous in supplying materials, they are parsimonious in one sense. At the end of the day the development of Sufic understanding makes real the effect of all that has gone before. Sufis do not supply, for the learner, materials, experiences even, which will be wasted. So, at the end of the day, everything fits into place. So finely is the economy of this teaching balanced that people are sure to benefit from what efforts have been expended. But if these efforts are not properly carried out, others, not the person who makes them, will be the beneficiaries.

THE BOOK OF THE BOOK

by Idries Shah

"This is a handsome, red-and-gold volume which is easy on the eye and weighs satisfactorily in the hand. It is a brief, dense, ancient tale of a book, of the book of that book, what it gave, and what people were able to take from it. The unalerted reader, turning page after page, may wonder if it is a joke.

"Actually it is – among other things – an extraordinary psychological test, in that it predicts the complete range of possible responses to itself."
Sunday Telegraph

"Beyond words" (*The Observer*); "Something new for the West" (*The Guardian*); "Tantalizing" (*World Medicine*); "Shattered the literary world" (*Irish Press*); "Astonishing" (*Sunday Mirror*); "Looks legit" (*The Arizona Republic*).

THE SUFIS

by Idries Shah

"Many forlorn puzzles in the world, which seemed to suggest that some great spiritual age somewhere in the Middle East had long since died and left indecipherable relics, suddenly come to organic life in this book."

Ted Hughes: *The Listener*

"Sufism is...'the inner secret teaching that is concealed within every religion.' The book has flashes of what (without intending to define the word) I can only call illumination."

D. J. Enright: *New Statesman*

"Fully authoritative" (*Afghanistan News*); "Important historically and culturally" (*Los Angeles Times*); "Incredibly rich in scope and fine detail" (*Psychology Today*); "The definitive statement of Sufism" (*Library Journal*); "Now its influence is spreading where long overdue" (*The American Scholar*); "More extraordinary the more it is studied" (*Encounter*); "Most comprehensively informative" (*New York Times Book Review*).

TALES OF THE DERVISHES

by Idries Shah

"These are teaching stories, spanning more than 1,000 years, from Persian, Arabic and Turkish traditional collections – published and in manuscript – and from oral sources, which include contemporary teaching centers; chosen and arranged by a Sufi to present to Westerners a Sufi view of life: one that challenges our intellectual assumptions at almost every point."

The Observer

"An astonishingly generous and liberating book… strikingly appropriate for our time and situation."

The Sunday Times

"Stories which equal, and sometimes surpass, in relevance, piquancy and humor, the best of the spiritual and ethical teachers of the West…sourcebook of authentic teaching-stories."

Kirkus Review

"Beautifully translated…equips men and women to make good use of their lives."

Professor James Kritzeck: *The Nation*

THE WAY OF THE SUFI
by Idries Shah

"The definitive account of ancient Sufi teaching. A great many common Western distortions and misinterpretations are cleared away, and much valuable source material anthologized."

Tribune

"A present for anyone who, though religious, finds the current orthodoxies unpalatable."

Times Literary Supplement

"Highly educative, basic course of study; intrinsic relevance to all."

The Hindu

"A key book...can assist to demonstrate other possible uses of the mind...gives new material on method, history, personnel, much of it from oral sources."

The Observer

SUFI STUDIES: EAST AND WEST

Edited by Professor L. F. Rushbrook Williams, CBE

"This assembly of learned papers by twenty-four world scholars of eminence...is a singular achievement. Not only does it gather together numerous respected names in the Islamic world of scholarship and letters of India, Pakistan, Afghanistan, Iran, Turkey and the Arab lands, but their individual contributions, mostly on Shah and his work during the past two decades, shows a depth of understanding and an ability to contribute which have caused this scholarly *festschrift* to be acclaimed in general as well as specialist journals of the East and West....

"Shah is certainly the best exponent of Sufi thought and teaching in its most comprehensive and authoritative forms that is to be found."

Islamic Culture

CARAVAN OF DREAMS

by Idries Shah

"One can read a story or two and be delighted. But the effect does not stop there. These stories adhere, return, seeming somehow to expand after reading into an area beyond outer consciousness. Like fine poems...like great poems...more than rewarding, and impossible to forget."

Tribune

"Like a fabled caravan from another time, this book travels great distances...re-stimulates the dream, by indicating real possibilities and practical alternatives to our present ways of operation; presenting not idle fantasies but signals from the tradition of known and tested activity; relevant, fruitful and urgent for our present society."

New Society

SEEKER AFTER TRUTH
by Idries Shah

A handbook, inviting the reader to reexamine the assumptions of his particular culture; assumptions which are responsible for his conditioning and his outlook on life.

"It is precisely because of the unreliability of vision, of memory, of wanting to believe, of induced belief...that the Sufis say that an objective perception must be acquired before even familiar things can be seen as they are."

Among the many assumptions questioned are: the objective worth of deep emotional feelings; the superiority of man's social habits over those of rats, and the origin of those habits; the evils of deceit.

"A book unlike anything our society has produced until recently, in its richness, its unexpectedness, its capacity to shock us into seeing ourselves as others see us."

Literary Review

THE MANIPULATED MIND
by Denise Winn

In this demystification of brainwashing, the author looks at the weaknesses (and the strengths) of the human mind and shows that, far from being a special subversive technique, brainwashing is the clever manipulation of a variety of influences that operate in all our lives.

"These techniques have always been used by armies, religions, cults and the police, everywhere... For us ordinary citizens, this is essential reading; a rapid, efficient survey of ideas and research that affect, that will increasingly affect, us all."

Doris Lessing: *New Society*

THE SPIRIT OF THE EAST
Sirdar Ikbal Ali Shah

Today the kinship of all religious thought and dogma is becoming more apparent to mankind – and the value of Oriental thought to the Occidental mind is obvious. Here is a selection from Muslim, Parsee, Hindu, Hebrew, Confucian and other sources, chosen not only for their spiritual worth but also the particular virtues of each creed which they represent.

The aim of this book is to introduce readers to the religious thought of the East, which – for reasons of language and other difficulties – they might otherwise have considered inaccessible.

REFLECTIONS

by Idries Shah

This selection of Idries Shah's own fables, aphorisms and teachings is now in its third edition and continues to be extremely popular.

Pocket-sized, it is immensely entertaining and at the same time offers an alternative view of our society that is both refreshing and profitable.

"More wisdom than I have found in any other books this year."
		Pat Williams: *Review of the Year*, BBC

"It seems to oblige the mind to scorn the satisfaction of going from A to B in favor of an approach from a different angle, taking in unsuspected territory."
		Evening News

TEACHINGS OF RUMI

THE MASNAVI
Abridged and translated by
E. H. Whinfield

Jalaluddin Rumi's great work, *The Masnavi*, was forty-three years in the writing. During the past seven hundred years, this book, called by Iranians "The Qur'an of Persian," a tribute paid to no other book, has occupied a central place in Sufism.

"*The Masnavi* is full of profound mysteries, and a most important book in the study of Sufism – mysteries which must, for the most part, be left to the discernment of the reader."
F. Hadland Davis

"To the Sufi, if not to anyone else, this book speaks from a different dimension, yet a dimension which is in a way within his deepest self."
Idries Shah

"The greatest mystical poet of any age."
                    Professor R. A. Nicolson

"It can well be argued that he is the supreme mystical poet of all mankind."
                    Professor A. J. Arberry

SPECIAL PROBLEMS IN THE STUDY OF SUFI IDEAS

by Idries Shah

This important monograph constitutes the whole text of Idries Shah's Seminar at Sussex University, fully annotated, indexed and with a bibliography and notes.

It knits together the available knowledge about Sufi thought and literature in its passage through many deforming influences, such as the development of cults, the misinterpretation by literalist scholars, and the fallacious comparisons of committed "specialists."

"Masterful essay...he has ably presented Sufism to the West and has conveyed its deep sense of reality to modern man..."

Professor A. Reza Arasteh:
Psychology of the Sufi Way, 1972

A Request

If you enjoyed this book, please review it on Amazon and Goodreads.

Reviews are an author's best friend.

To stay in touch with news on forthcoming editions of Idries Shah works, please sign up for the mailing list:

 http://bit.ly/ISFlist

And to follow him on social media, please go to any of the following links:

 https://twitter.com/idriesshah

 https://www.facebook.com/IdriesShah

 http://www.youtube.com/idriesshah999

 http://www.pinterest.com/idriesshah/

 http://bit.ly/ISgoodreads

 http://idriesshah.tumblr.com

 https://www.instagram.com/idriesshah/

http://idriesshahfoundation.org

www.ingramcontent.com/pod-product-compliance
Lightning Source LLC
Chambersburg PA
CBHW071408160426
42813CB00092B/3428/J